Farming

Tatiana Tomljanovic

Weigl

CALGARY

www.weigl.com

Published by Weigl Educational Publishers Limited
6325 10 Street SE
Calgary, Alberta T2H 2Z9

Library of Congress Cataloging-in-Publication Data

Tomljanovic, Tatiana
      Farming / Tatiana Tomljanovic.

(Linking Canadian Communities)
Includes index.
ISBN 978-1-55388-377-7 (bound)
ISBN 978-1-55388-378-4 (pbk.)

      1. Agriculture--Canada--Juvenile literature. 2. Agriculture--Economic
aspects--Canada--Juvenile literature. 3. Agriculture--Canada--History--
Juvenile literature. I. Title. II. Series.
HD1783.T65 2007   j338.10971   C2007-902263-4

Printed in the United States of America
1 2 3 4 5 6 7 8 9 11 10 09 08 07

Editor
Heather C. Hudak
Design
Warren Clark

All of the Internet URLs given in the book were valid at the time of publication. However, due to the
dynamic nature of the Internet, some addresses may have changed, or sites may have ceased to exist
since publication. While the author and publisher regret any inconvenience this may cause readers,
no responsibility for any such changes can be accepted by either the author or the publisher.

Photograph Credits: Great Western Railway Ltd.: page 6.
Every reasonable effort has been made to trace ownership and to obtain permission to reprint copyright
material. The publishers would be pleased to have any errors or omissions brought to their attention so
that they may be corrected in subsequent printings.

We acknowledge the financial support of the Government of Canada through the Book Publishing
Industry Development Program (BPIDP) for our publishing activities.

Contents

What is a Community?

A community is a place where people live, work, and play together. There are large and small communities.

Small communities are also called rural communities. These communities have fewer people and less traffic than large communities. There is plenty of open space.

Large communities are called towns or cities. These are urban communities. They have taller buildings and more cars, stores, and people than rural communities.

Canada has many types of communities. Some have forests for logging. Others have farms. There are also fishing, energy, **manufacturing**, and mining communities.

Types of Canadian Communities

FARMING COMMUNITIES
- use the land to grow crops, such as wheat, barley, canola, fruits, and vegetables
- some raise livestock, such as cattle, sheep, and pigs

ENERGY COMMUNITIES
- found near energy sources, such as water, natural gas, oil, coal, and uranium
- have **natural resources**
- provide power for homes and businesses

FISHING COMMUNITIES
- found along Canada's 202,080 kilometres of coastline
- fishers catch fish, lobster, shrimp, and other underwater life

Real Canadian Communities

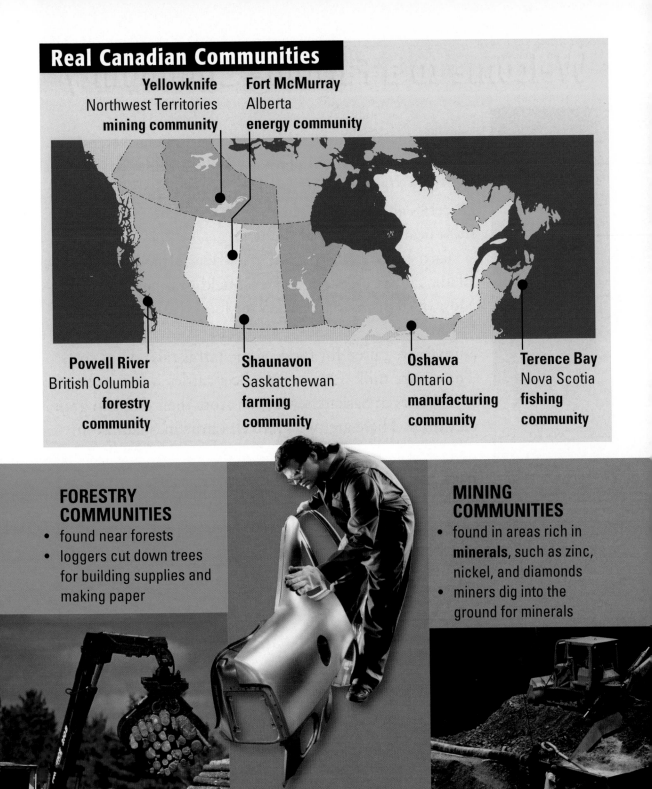

Yellowknife
Northwest Territories
mining community

Fort McMurray
Alberta
energy community

Powell River
British Columbia
**forestry
community**

Shaunavon
Saskatchewan
**farming
community**

Oshawa
Ontario
**manufacturing
community**

Terence Bay
Nova Scotia
**fishing
community**

FORESTRY COMMUNITIES
- found near forests
- loggers cut down trees for building supplies and making paper

MINING COMMUNITIES
- found in areas rich in **minerals**, such as zinc, nickel, and diamonds
- miners dig into the ground for minerals

MANUFACTURING COMMUNITIES
- use natural resources to make a finished product
- finished products include cars and computers

Welcome to a Farming Community

Shaunavon is a farming community in Saskatchewan. It is a small town of about 2,000 people. Shaunavon has a few stores that sell products. These include groceries and farm supplies and equipment. Farmers from nearby depend on the town.

Farmers near Shaunavon grow wheat, flax, oats, barley, alfalfa, clover, chickpeas, lentils, field peas, and canola. Most of these grains are used for food. Farmers also grow hay for animal feed. Some farmers keep livestock. These animals are raised for food. Some farms raise dairy cows. They make milk. Others have beef cattle, swine, or sheep.

Farmers in Saskatchewan can store their crops in grain **elevators**. There are two grain elevators in Shaunavon.

Trains carry crops and livestock across the country to other communities.

First-hand Account

Saskatchewan

Shaunavon

My name is Lauren. I live on a farm outside of Shaunavon. There are lots of little towns like Shaunavon in Saskatchewan. When I first moved here, we passed through many towns before reaching our farm.

My dad is a farmer. He grows wheat. In August and September, my dad **harvests** his crops. Then he brings the wheat to the grain elevators. My mom goes to town with him to shop. Shaunavon's main street is wide. It has no traffic lights.

I ride the bus to school each day. Some of the kids in my class are from town. Others live on farms. My classmates who ride on the bus eat their lunch at school. I eat lunch with my friend Luba. Her family lives on the farm nearest ours.

Think About It

Compare Shaunavon to your community.

- Is the environment the same or different?
- How is it the same? How is it different?

The Farming Industry

Farmers who grow and harvest crops are part of the farming industry. Farmers who have livestock are also part of this industry. The farming industry includes factories and other businesses that make food products from crops and livestock.

The farming industry is one of the most important industries on the Canadian Prairies. Saskatchewan, Alberta, and Manitoba are the Prairie Provinces. Farming makes many jobs for people in prairie communities. Most farmers on the Prairies grow grains. Fruits and vegetables grow well in other parts of Canada.

Modern machinery helps increase productivity in farming communities.

Timeline

2000 YEARS AGO

Canada's Aboriginal Peoples begin planting crops of corn, beans, and squash.

1701

Jethro Tull invents the seed-drill, the first farming machine.

1850

The John Deere Company manufactures 10,000 iron ploughs. Ploughs cut, lift, and turn over soil.

On the Prairies, farmers work in the fields growing and harvesting crops. They take grains to be stored in elevators. Later, grain is moved from the elevators to mills and factories that process the grains into food products.

Wheat, flax, oats, barley, and canola are grains grown in Canada. Wheat is used to make bread. Canola is used to make cooking oil. The Prairies often are called Canada's "bread basket." The Prairies are a main source of the grains used to make bread.

There are many cattle farms in Canada. These farms raise cows for beef. Farmers have other types of livestock in Canada, too. They may have bison, swine, or ostrich. These animals are sold for food or clothing.

Food products from the farming industry are used in communities across Canada.

1880
The building of railways helps the Canadian farming industry. Crops are moved across the country faster and more easily.

1940s
Most farmers use machines to farm instead of horses and cattle.

2004
Canada ships farming products worth $16 billion to the United States.

Canola Crushing Process

One of the crops farmers grow around Shaunavon is canola. It is different from wheat, oats, and barley. Canola is an oilseed crop. The seeds are crushed to produce cooking oil. Canola oil can also be made into margarine and whipped dessert topping.

Shaunavon does not have a crushing plant. Farmers send their crops to other communities for crushing. The nearest crushing plant is in Saskatoon, Saskatchewan. There are many crushing plants in Saskatchewan, Alberta, Ontario, and Quebec. Most plants can crush more than 6,000 **tonnes** of canola per year. The crushing plant in Nipawin, Saskatchewan, can crush 104,000 tonnes of canola per year.

Canola is one of Saskatchewan's most important crops.

Canola Crushing Process

Canola is harvested.

↓

Canola is sent to an elevator for storage.

↓

Canola is sent to a crushing plant.

↓

Canola seeds are crushed to produce oil.

→ The leftover seeds are mixed with feed for cattle and chickens.

→ The oil is refined into thick, thin, clear, or dark oil.

↓

Some of the oil is used for cooking.

↓

Some of the oil is made into margarine and other products.

↓

Canola products are shipped all over Canada and the world.

Canada's Farmlands Map

Farmers grow many kinds of crops. Some farmers grow wheat or barley. About 68 million **hectares** of land in Canada are used for farming. This map shows the different kinds of farming in Canada. It also shows where some farming communities are found.

Legend

Land used for farming

Cattle

Fruits and vegetables

Grains, including wheat and barley

Hogs

Poultry

Dairy

Surface crops, such as potatoes and soy

U.S.A.

Yukon Territory

• Whitehorse

Northwest Territories

Nunavut

Yellowknife

C A N A D A

Alberta

Saskatchewan

British Columbia

Edmonton

Pacific Ocean

Victoria

Regina

U N I T E D   S T A T E S
O F   A M E R I C A

N

0   500 kilometres
0   500 miles

Iqaluit

Labrador Sea

Hudson Bay

Manitoba

Newfoundland
and Labrador

St.
John's

Quebec

Prince Edward
Island

Ontario

New
Brunswick

Nova
Scotia

Charlottetown

Winnipeg

Quebec City

Ottawa ★

Fredericton

Halifax

Toronto

Atlantic Ocean

Careers

About 2 million Canadians work in jobs that are related to farming. Many work in food processing companies, grocery stores, and restaurants.

The farming industry needs other businesses. Some people help make and ship products. Equipment and ovens are needed to turn grains into food products. Trucks, trains, and ships are needed to carry Canada's grain to other places.

Farmers plant and harvest crops. They make up a small part of the farming industry. Other workers depend on farmers to provide raw materials for the finished products.

Butcher shops and bakeries carry fresh bread and meat made from farm products.

Elevator agents monitor, or manage, the amount and type of grain that is stored in the elevators. Later, the grain is loaded onto trains and trucks. Then, it is shipped to flour mills and crushing plants. It is also sent to other factories that make grains into flour and oil.

Flour and oil are sold to grocery stores, bakers, and cooks. Bakers use flour to make different types of breads, cakes, and other foods. Most baked foods are made with flour. Cookies, bagels, muffins, and pastries are made with flour.

Ranchers care for livestock. They feed the animals daily. They also keep records of the animals and brand them. Dairy cows are milked using machines. Some animals are sent by truck to the market. They are used for food.

Baking foods from farm products, such as wheat, has become a major industry in Canada.

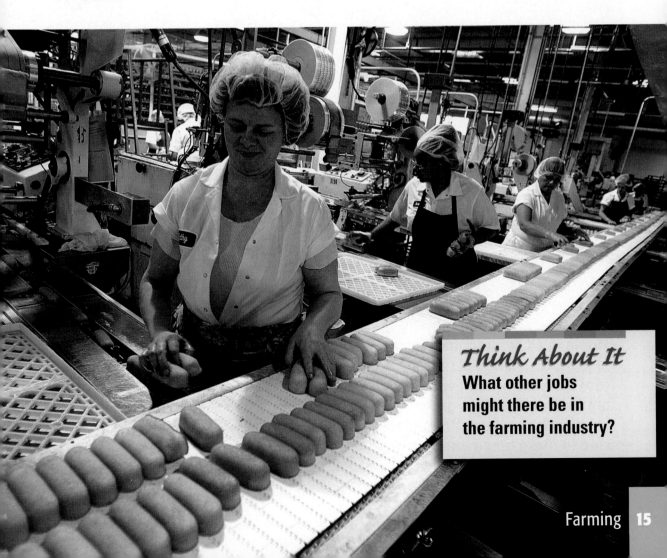

Think About It
What other jobs might there be in the farming industry?

Links Between Communities

Everyone is part of a community. It may be a village, a town, or a city. Communities are linked to one another. Each Canadian community uses goods that link it to other communities. Goods are things people grow, make, or gather to use or sell.

A forestry community makes lumber for construction. The wood may be shipped to another community to build houses or furniture.

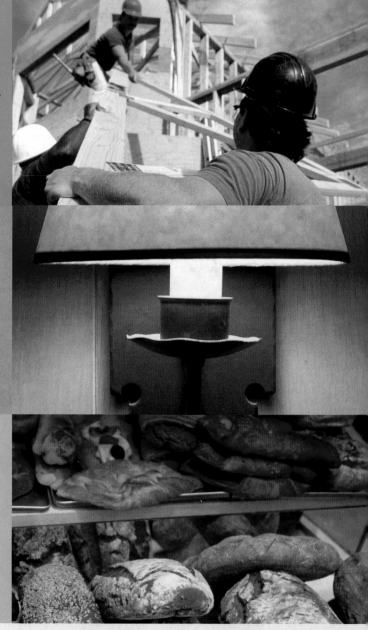

Energy communities produce natural gas, oil, and other types of energy, such as wind, solar, and hydro. Other communities use this energy to power their homes and vehicles.

Dairy products and meats come from farming communities that raise cattle and other animals. People in all communities drink milk products and eat meat from these communities. Many farming communities grow crops such as wheat. Wheat is used to make bread and pastries.

These goods may be fish, grains, cars, and paper products. Communities depend on one another for goods and services. A service is useful work that is done to meet the needs of others. People are linked when they use the goods and services provided by others.

Manufacturing communities make products such as cars and trucks. They also make airplanes, ships, and trains that are used to transport, or move, people and goods from one place to another. Transportation services help communities build links.

Fishing communities send fish to stores to be bought by people in other places. In Canada, most fish is caught off the Pacific or Atlantic coast. People living on farms or in cities across the country buy the fish at stores.

Diamonds, gold, and potash can be mined. These items are sent from mining communities to other parts of the country. A diamond might be set in a ring for a person in another community.

Think About It
In your community, what goods and services help meet your family's needs and wants?

The Environment and the Community

Many Canadian farmers use fertilizers and pesticides to grow their crops. Fertilizers add **nutrients** to the soil. Pesticides kill insects that eat crops. There are **chemicals** in fertilizers and pesticides. Chemicals can help crops grow. Too many pesticides may harm the soil so that crops do not grow well.

Some farmers use crop dusters to fertilize their crops.

Think About It

Some farmers do not believe in using chemicals. This is called organic farming. Organic food costs more to buy. It does not add chemicals to the environment. Do you think that organic farming or farming that uses pesticides is better?

Canadian farmers use fewer pesticides than most countries. This is partly due to the weather. Canada has cold winters. There also is a short growing season. Insects cannot live in the cold prairie winters. Canada has fewer insects than warmer countries.

Shaunavon's water comes from an **aquifer**. Fertilizers and pesticides can pollute Shaunavon's water supply. Waste from livestock can also pollute water. The water in lakes, rivers, and puddles is connected. Each day, water **evaporates**. Then, it returns to the ground in the form of rain. This process is called the water cycle. When chemicals are added to soil or the ground, the chemicals enter water in the soil. That water flows to other places, such as creeks.

Eco-friendly Pesticides

Researchers and scientists are making pesticides that do not harm the environment. These pesticides kill insect pests. They do not leave dangerous chemicals on the crops or in the soil.

Brain Teasers

Test your knowledge by trying to answer these brain teasers.

Q **What are pesticides?**

A Pesticides are chemicals that kill insects that eat crops.

Q **Name three types of communities in Canada.**

A Canada has forestry communities, farming communities, fishing communities, energy communities, mining communities, and manufacturing communities.

Q **What two things link communities?**

A Goods and services link different communities together.

Q **What products can be made from wheat? What products can be made from canola?**

A Wheat can be used to make bread, pastries, and baked foods. Canola can be used to make cooking oil, margarine, and whipped topping.

Q **What is the difference between a rural and an urban community?**

A A rural community has plenty of open space and few people. An urban community has taller buildings and more people.

Q **Where is Shaunavon?**

A Shaunavon is located in Saskatchewan.

Choosing Soil Activity

Soil is very important to crop growth. Some crops grow better in moist soil. Some crops grow better in dry soil. What kind of soil is needed to grow alfalfa? Try this experiment to find out.

Materials

- 3 soil samples (1 litre each) such as sand, potting soil, clay, and topsoil
- 3 plastic tubs
- alfalfa seeds
- water
- sunlight
- marker

Procedure

1. Put each soil sample in a plastic tub.

2. Use the marker to label each tub.

3. Plant a few seeds of alfalfa in the middle of each tub.

4. Put all three tubs in the same spot by a window that lets sunlight in.

5. Water the soil whenever it starts to become dry.

6. After two weeks, check to see which soil is best for growing alfalfa.

Further Research

Many books and websites provide information on farming communities. To learn more about farming communities, borrow books from the library, or surf the Internet.

Books

Most libraries have computers that connect to a database for researching information. If you input a key word, you will be provided with a list of books in the library that contain information on that topic. Non-fiction books are arranged numerically, using their call number. Fiction books are organized alphabetically by the author's last name.

Websites

The World Wide Web is also a good source of information. Reliable websites usually include government sites, educational sites, and online encyclopedias.

Learn more about the community of Shaunavon by visiting the town website at **www.shaunavon.com**.

To find out about the canola industry in Canada and the different products that can be made from the crop, check out **www.canola-council.org**.

Check out thousands of photos of grain elevators in Saskatchewan and other parts of Canada at **www.grainelevators.ca**.

Words to Know

aquifer: underground layer of water

chemicals: substances produced by scientists

elevators: storage buildings for grains

evaporates: turns from a liquid to a vapor

harvests: gathers a crop

hectares: areas of 10,000 square metres

manufacturing: making a large amount of an item using machines

minerals: inorganic substances that are obtained through mining

natural resources: materials found in nature, such as water, soil, and forests, that can be used by people

nutrients: things that are needed by plants for life and growth

tonnes: a unit of measurement equal to 1,000 kilograms

Index